A
Revelation
of
Poetry

A
Revelation
of

Poetry

Carol E. Carradine - Madison

ARPress
ILLUMINATING IDEAS
EMPOWERING VOICES

ARPress
45 Dan Road Suite 5
Canton MA 02021

Hotline: 1(888) 821-0229
Fax: 1(508) 545-7580

Ordering Information:

Quantity sales. Special discounts are available on quantity purchases by corporations, associations, and others. For details, contact the publisher at the address above.

Printed in the United States of America.

ISBN-13:   Paperback   979-8-89356-846-2
              eBook   979-8-89356-847-9

Library of Congress Control Number: 2024908978

Table of Contents

PREFACE

God inspired these poems. I want to give Him praise and thanks for awakening a talent that was dominant in me. The author and Finisher of my faith, the Lord and Savior Jesus Christ, revealed these poems.

This poetry has been a blessing to my soul, as God has used me to write it. I present A Revelation of Poetry with the intended purpose of blessing someone's soul.

I AM THE FUTURE!

(A poem of self-awareness)
Psalm 139:14; Genesis 1:26, 28; 2:7; Romans 8:37

I am the Future

I face it with excitement, anticipation, and enthusiasm, and I walk into it with grace and eagerness!

I am the Future

I look to every day with readiness to be a great asset to myself, my race, my nation, and all people!

I am the Future

I will make a difference for my generation. I am the black child Dr. King spoke of who will stand hand and hand with the white child equally. The reason is that together we can stand and not fall!

I Am the Future

I Am the Change

I am the unique creation of God. He has equipped me with everything I need for the Future. It all lies within me. The Future is already waiting to transform me. I am somebody. I am the Perfect Creation of God!

CALL ME! I HEAR YOU!

(A poem of help)
Revelation 3:20; Isaiah 30:21, 53:4, 5, Matthew 7:7

You are called Father, My God, Holy Ghost, Jesus, Jehovah, My Rock, and Savior, yes! You are all these names. You are whatever I need to be at any given time! Whenever you call, I hear that you are the answer to whatever I ask. Whenever there is sickness or pain, there You are the healer. Whatever is required, You are the provider. You said to call Me; I hear You!

Whenever there is discouragement, read my word; it encourages. Whenever you're in doubt, Sing, Worship, and Praise me. It's your only way out! Call Me, I hear You!

Whenever you are lonely or sad, think of My Son Jesus! Who gave his life, that you may have everlasting life. And this will make you glad if you're in sin and at your wit's end. If every door seems shut and there's no way out! Repent my child, and accept your salvation. So now, let's rejoice and be happy and give a big shout! Call Me, I hear You!

Whenever you're weak

Be strong in the Lord,

And in the power of His Might. So then, there you'll find it!

Strength in his word that you seek. I am the Alpha, the Omega. The Beginning, The End. God is which was and which is still to come. The Almighty!

COMMITTED TO YOU

(A poem of commitment)
I Samuel 15:33; Romans 5:1, 2

God,
I am committed to you,
To do all things you've called me to do.

You said obedience is better than sacrifice,
I want you to be pleased with the direction of my life.

Serving you is my heart's desire,
Knowing that you love me makes everything worthwhile.

I will let my faith rise!
I know your knowledge to keep me wise!

I will work hard to conquer the test!
I will study my word because in it will find rest!

MY KING, MY QUEEN

You were born from royalty from the kingdom of God
You are my daughter who was born a Queen
Whom I loan to my son, who is a King

Only my son, who is a King, never realized he is a King
Now because my son, who is a King, never realized he is a King

He did not know how to honor and respect my Queen
So now, my daughter, a Queen, could never realize she is a Queen

My King, My Queen, God created you to become a team

To fulfill your purpose from birth, to represent me throughout the earth My King, My Queen, I know your worth; I gave it to you to honor and

respect each other here on earth

It is you, my daughter, who is my Queen, and you, my son, who is my King

to realize who you are

My son and my daughter know that you are from a royal priest

hood, the Kingdom of God

You are a King, and You are a Queen

A FRIEND

(A poem of friendship)
John 15-13, 14, 15

You are a person who will
Always be special to me!
Your love and affection have
Been precious to me!

To hear you say my name
Make it seems as though nothing
Has changed!

Your smile and your laughter fills
My heart
And it seems we are never
Apart

Just know in your heart, in my life
God, no one could ever erase you
I will never forget all (our) special days!
You will remain in my heart now, forever, and always!

DON'T GIVE UP

(A poem of encouragement)
John 14:18; Isaiah 40:31; 1 Peter 5:6,7

God, you taught me
I must trust You!
All the trials and tribulations,
You've brought me through!

The mountains and hills
Were so hard to climb!
But You were there behind me all the time!

When times get hard and
I wanted to stop
You kept on telling me,
Don't forget I love you a lot

Don't ever give up,
Trust in me!
Always, remember in me,
You have the Victory!

A PLACE SO SERENE, SO BEAUTIFUL

(A poem of comfort)
Matthew 11:28, 29; Ecclesiastes 3:1,8; Revelation 7:14,17

O' what a beautiful place I see,
My soul is finally free
My spirit soaring on high
My Savior, I'm sitting by
No more suffering and no more pain,
My soul, Yes, the Lord, he has gained
Think of me up here in the clouds so blue,
And knowing everyone, I'll be waiting
With open arms for you
So, celebrate! Be joyous in spirit and soul,
Because of My Savior's face, I do behold
Now I sit at my Savior's feet,
In a beautiful place where I long to be
Assured this is my last move,
I have accepted and know
That I am approved
Oh, what a place, A BEAUTIFUL PLACE!

SOMEONE TO LISTEN

(A poem of consolation)
1 John 5:14; Philippians 4:7, 2 Thessalonians 3:16

My spirit was heavy,
In despair today!
I needed someone to listen to,
What I had to say!

You were there and
You listened very quietly!
Never, ever saying,
How you thought it should be!

I talked, and I prayed
Till my soul found release!
With your spirit all around me,
I knew in my heart; that I had found peace.

LORD IS MY HELPER

(A poem for help)
Psalm 23

Oh, where is my helper?
The Lord is my shepherd
Now, why should I want!
Lord, I am out of control,
My life, I cannot master!
I want to lie down
In your green pastures!
My soul has been like a deep dark hole,
But you lead me beside your quiet waters,
And You restore my soul!
I am miss-guided throughout the day
With decisions, I cannot make
But then you come and guide me
In the path of righteousness for your name's sake!
It is tough to talk
In courage, I must walk!
There is not much of me left
As I go through this valley
Of the shadow of death!

Satan is on each side; you see
I am looking for protection to help me!
I will fear no evil because I know you are with me
Your rod and staff comfort me,
Everyone is against me!
But you have prepared a table before me
in the presence of my enemies!
When everyday doors are shut and closed
You anoint my head with oil and let my cup overflow!
If confusion and strife consume my day

Undoubtedly, your goodness and love will follow me
All the days of my life!
When I cannot hide my face ever
I will dwell in your house Lord forever,
Amen.

YOU ARE WELCOME

(A poem of welcome)

Come into the Holy of Holies
Enter by the blood of the lamb!
Come into his presence by singing
Enter the throne of God!
You are welcome to lift holy hands,
To praise him and do a holy dance!
You are welcome to worship and pray
And lift Jesus in your own way
You are welcome to sing a song
We have the liberty to praise him all day long!
If you feel like testifying about the things he has done for you,
Come on! Speak out! And let us know too!
We don't need to say,
That you are welcome in God's house just today!
So, kick off your shoes and relax your feet!
Let the Holy Ghost move you
To the sound of the beat!
Because one should see
We are free!
To be in God's House
Anywhere you might be!
We are not here for a show
But I want all to know!
That Jesus has been waiting for you to walk through the door!
I want to tell you that
You are welcome and blessed here today!
Jesus is here in every way!

O, SINNER

(A poem to re-think)
Proverbs 8:36; 28:13; Romans 6:23

O wretched sinner, yes, it's me
Going through life thinking I am free!

I was living life in the way I thought was right!
God showed me his perfect light!

Sinned, I live every day
Until this voice said, this is not the way!

This voice I ignored; I did do!
I kept on living like I wanted to.

Trapped in sin, I could not see!
This perfect plan God had for me!

I never knew my life
Was not mine
That I was born to be
God's all the time

I thought life was
This big, terrific thing
Until I understood all the
Love Jesus could bring!

Life changes constantly
Day by day
Leading and directing me toward a better way!

THE REASON FOR THE SEASON

(A poem of gifts from God)
Exodus 1:1, 5; John 3:16; I Corinthians 2:4, 13; Galatians 5:22, 28

As we trim the tree and hang the lights that shine so bright, I hear Jesus saying, what about Me?

As we sit around the tree to unwrap gifts, we're so excited to see I hear Jesus saying, What about Me?

We have set the table for the food that we will eat today!
Yet, how could we forget to pray?

I hear Jesus saying, "Wait one minute, there's something I must say! Oh, my children, this is not the way"!

God ordained from the beginning that I would be!
Your Savior to the world to bring salvation and give you eternity!

I am the tree of life; I am the one to shine bright in your life plug into me, and you will surely see all the things I have for thee!

As you bring your ornaments to me, take all the fruit of the

spirit and hang them carefully. Bring me love, joy, peace, patience, kindness, goodness, faithfulness, gentleness, and self-control.

Believe in me; this tree of life stands tall with strong branches and green leaves! To all the world! I am your King!

THE SPLENDOR OF IT ALL

(A poem of God's glory)

I sit far off in a quiet place,
Just looking around and admiring your nature
With a beautiful thought of
The glory of your face!

Even with the sounds of silence in my ear
I can hear!

The wind blowing through the trees,
And the birds singing in the sky
Just imagining to myself!
But never ask the reason why?

How excellent is your work?
With the water so blue,
And the grass so green,
With the air so fresh!
You knew what this earth needed best

I will never understand. God is so amazing to me!
The skill of His hands in this world we see!
But as I look at the splendor in the earth,
It's very apparent to me!

THE FLOW OF LOVE

(A poem of love)
I John 4:6,8; I John 4:16, 17, 18, 19: Romans 8:38, 39

Your love is like a river
That flows through my soul!
Running deep and wide
All through my inside.

How addicting to me!
I can't break free!
With love so strong,
That has lasted so long!

What a joy I have found!
Since your love has been around!

Your love has healed all
The hurts inside of me!
Which has brought me more
Closer to serving thee!

Your love is something
I don't want to lose!
Never again in life
Will I have to choose!

I looked all around
And no one could pass the test!
But when I found you,
You were the BEST!

BECAUSE YOU ARE MINE

(A poem for marriage)
Genesis 2:2-1; Proverbs 31: II, 12; Ephesians 5:25, 28, 31

I love you because you're mine
I love you because you are kind

I love you because you're sweet
I love you because all my needs you meet

I love you because your love is free
I love you because you're always there for me

I love you because you're a part of my life
I love you because I am your wife

I love you because you understand me
I love you because you believe; you see

I love you because we are a part of God's plan
I love you because you know how to take a stand

I love you because you never walked away
I love you because; your love you confess every day

I love you because God saved the best for me
I love you because our love will last through eternity

THE CROSS

(A poem for salvation)
John 3:16; Luke 23:26-16; Revelation 1:18; 9: 1

Jesus' arms are open
wide on the cross!
Telling you to come, all who are lost.

Even though He hung high
in the sky!
Jesus' arms reach out for you,
that you may not be passed by!

As His blood and water fall
to the ground! He's interceding to the Father
that you will be found.

Let not what He's done
be lost in vain!
The cross was not easy
He had some pain!

But for you, He bowed His head
and gave up the Ghost!
Because with all his heart,
He loved you the most!

Jesus went to hell and
took back what was mine!
Brought back the keys
for all mankind!

Three days later, He arose
transformed and brand new
With a new way of life, just for you!

WHO AM I?

(A poem about knowing who you are)
Psalm 139:14 Galatians 2:20

I am just another person placed here on earth
Is there a reason and a purpose for my birth?

As I wonder who I am all through my mind
The spirit inside says that I am one of a kind.

Who am I? Is my life remarkable in some unique way?
Was I placed here on earth with something important to say?

Did God create me with a purpose and a plan?
Am I skillfully designed for a reason with his own hands?

Who am I?

God gave me a mind, body, and soul
I know I must keep in control.

Who am I?

I must remove myself and how I feel
It is God's plan and purpose that he will reveal

Who am I?

Am I the person who stands in my way?
Making wrong choices and decisions every day
God tell me, please, what path should I take?

Who am I?

GIVE ME A CHANCE

(A poem for renewing the mind)
Psalm: 91; 139; Proverbs 3:6

Give Me a chance,
To turn your life into what I have ordained it to be!
When you entered out of your mother's womb,
You were free!

Give Me a chance,
Because you are free to choose
I will give you strength and
I will never let you lose

Give Me a chance,
To let you see that your life is a script
that God has written!
With much guidance and direction,
It is never hidden!

Give Me a chance,
That you may dwell in the secret place of the Highest.
Let me bless and anoint you with My Love!
And you never have to ask Me why!

Give Me a chance,
To cover you under My wings
So, you will learn about the protection,
I bring

Give Me a chance,
To give my angels charge over thee!
To help you in whatever situation you might be
Learn how to seek My face!
And I shall keep thee in all thy ways!

SPECIAL TO ME

(A poem for togetherness)
Proverbs 18:22; Genesis 2:24; Ephesians 5:25, 28, 31

You are special to me!
More than I thought you could ever be!

You are so thoughtful and kind!
I know just why God made you mine!

We have been through many things together.
But our love has survived all kinds of weather.

Words are not your specialty.
But I know in my heart that you give your love warmly!

We have grown to know what love is,
Even though it has taken many years.

You are a great husband and father too!
I thank God every day and night for you!
I know He is still molding you!

Together we have grown in time.
We have been together like a good old fashion wine!

This marriage has been an excellent experience for us!
It has taught us both how to trust!

I love you, and you love me.
Our love is the way it shall always be!

HEAL MY MIND

(A poem for healing)
Psalms 103:2. 3; 147:3; Jeremiah 30:17; 1 Peter 2:24

Jesus, my mind needs healing,
This world is just a big illusion
That brings on much confusion!

Heal my mind because I think,
I am going crazy!
This pain is making me feel a little hazy!
Satan doesn't want to let me go!
Please help me to decide which way to go!

I am sick of the sin
What's happening in my life!
It's cutting and stabbing me
Like a very sharp knife!

I am sick of this tugging
going on inside of my soul
Trying to prevent me
from reaching my goal!

Heal me in Your holy name!
With Your word, my mind, I will proclaim!
I pray in Jesus' precious name

PRAISING YOU!

(A poem for praise and worship)
Psalms 100; 105: 1, 2, 3; 107:8

I worship You
in the beauty of Your holiness.
Let heaven and earth
rejoice in Your fullness.

I will sing out loud.
My voice I will raise!
For You are great,
And greatly to be praised!

I will show forth
Your salvation from day to day.
Honoring and glorifying
Your name in every way!

No rocks or trees
Shall praise you in place of me!
Because I promise
To worship and praise you continuously!
Amen

OPEN ARMS

(A poem of embracement)
Romans 5:8; 8:38. 39; Matthew 27

Jesus' arms are always
stretched out wide
Waiting for you to come and embrace him
with all your love that's inside!

Jesus understands your hurt and painful cries
Who could understand it better than him?
Jesus' body nailed to the cross,
Pulled from limb to limb.

With each drop of blood that fell!
It gave us a new direction away from hell!

Jesus bowed his head
and gave up the Ghost
He told us all,
Who he loved the most!

SPIRIT

(A poem of the spirit)
I Corinthians 2: 11.12; Luke 11:13; John J.1:26; Psalm 118:6

God, You are always nearby!
Telling my spirit never to fear!

Your spirit sends my heart love!
That comes from heaven above!

Loving You is easy, you see!
You are a spirit just like ME!

THE SPIRIT INSIDE

(A poem of rest)
Jeremiah 31:3; John 14:18; Psalm 32:8

It is so awesome to me
How real You are!
Someone whose eyes cannot see!
But with a Spirit that's real
That is moving inside of me!
It's hard to comprehend,
Just what You've become to me!
I could never have imagined
it in my mind!
All this precious love, You
had all the time.
You have never left me
comfortless!
You have embraced me with Your rest!
Your guidance and direction
is always nearby.
Instructing me with Your words,
To never fear!
How could I live
Without You in my life?
On my own!
I could never live in a world of strife!
My assurance with You has your peace.
I am trusting and believing in Your power and love.
Knowing it will bring a sweet release.
I am living in this world today!
That's very important to me!

THE FIGHT

(A poem of victory)
II Corinthians 10:3, 6; Ephesians 6:10, 18

I had to fight with satan. He taunted and teased me so!
It was a vicious battle; that turned into a war!
We were fighting in the spirit world
He wanted to keep my soul! But my coach, who is Jesus, wouldn't let him
He said fight toward your goal!
I was down for the count. Satan shouted very loudly, "You're trapped here in SIN"!
But my coach, who is Jesus, said, " Get up and WIN, WIN, WIN!"
So let's turn this fight around; let's crush him in the ground!
I taught you how to fight! Now put your armor on
and fight with all your MIGHT!

ONLY YOU

(A poem of understanding)
Psalms 1:139

Who could know the depths?
Of my heart and soul so completely!
Who could know the exact thoughts?
Of my mind that runs so deeply!

Only You! O God, who looks down on me!
You know my direction before the day begins.
Your spirit leads me and keeps me from sin!

O Your Spirit leads me throughout the day!
You are shaping and forming me in Your special way.
O who could know what I needed the most
Only You, O precious God of Host!

WOMEN OF VICTORY

(A poem of victory)
I Corinthians 15:57; 1 John 5:4; Luke 24:22, 24

Stand tall, Stand Proud!
For yes, it is you, my daughters
To whom I have called!
Women of victory
It's time for the wall of Jericho to come tumbling down
Put faith into work
And spread my word all around
Women of victory
Stand in unity
Coming together
Representing Me your Savior and Lord
Women of victory
I have anointed you to set the captives free
Ministering salvation, repentance, restoration, deliverance
God has called it to be!
Women of victory,
Pray in the soul
Tell my people of my love and
All the beautiful blessings I have in store
Women of victory,
You shall give birth to new beginnings
You shall birth forth
New life.

New life in your church
New life in your home
New life in your community
God has created a brand-new life for the people all around you
You shall birth out of you
The purpose of life
That is to lift your Savior's name and proclaim him to everyone
Women of victory, it is God's will to be done!

OPEN EYES

John 3:16

I thank God for letting
me see!
A new way of life just
for me!

Now I must let go of this
world of strife.
So, I can live like Jesus,
in His perfect life.

Now I understand who I am!
My life was saved by this perfect Lamb!

So, this is what life is all
about
Informing me if I don't choose
Jesus, there's no way out!

Amen

JESUS DIET

This diet includes five essential words. They must be included in this diet every day for the best effectiveness.

Remember these five words: prayer, scripture, obedience, sacrifice, and commitment.

Stick to this diet, and you will accomplish an effective weight loss. Always remember your ingredients.

* Prayer—Every morning, pray in the spirit, asking for strength, willpower, encouragement, and guidance. These ingredients will get you started for the next step.

* Scriptures—After praying, add the word of God. Mix it in with these Scriptures. (The joy of the Lord is my strength. I can do all things through Jesus Christ, who strengthens me). (Add more scriptures as needed)

* Obedience—After adding prayer and scripture, stir in some obedience. Make sure you have obeyed by praying and reading the scriptures. Now throw in some listening. Let Jesus move in his direction. Never add or take away anything without his permission.

* Sacrifice—Now pour in many cups of sacrifice, and get ready to put in some things, like less food and more exercise. (Always remember Jesus' sacrifice on the cross; He gave up His life for you. Remember the sweat and the pain of carrying the cross to Calvary. Remember the victory in the end. (Add some fasting)

* Commitment—After using all of the following ingredients, please don't forget the commitment component. As we are committed to Christ, let us also be committed to ourselves to ensure that what we set out to do is accomplished. And through this commitment, God is glorified in spirit, soul, and body.

I FEEL

(A Poem of Transformation)

I feel your loneliness,
The void and emptiness,
That great big hole inside your soul.
I will take your spirit, and I will mold.

Take my love and embrace it with my rest!
For I am your God, I know what is best!

I am the potter, and you are on my wheel!
I am shaping and molding you for my perfect will!
As you spin around and around in this making of clay!
I am removing and straightening things that may stand in your way.

I see each teardrop that falls from your eyes.
I noticed all the restless nights that have passed you by.
There have been thoughts, memories, and reminders of the present and past.
I will uplift and sustain you with a love that will last.

There are many times in life we don't understand what we see!
There are many hurts and tribulations throughout life.
But know I have what's best for thee!

No one in this world could love you like me!
I know every hurt, every pain, loneliness, reminders, and memories.
I hold them very carefully!

Everything in life is a part of a plan.
But with each episode that comes our way!
Within your heart, always know it will teach and keep you for a perfect day!

THIS DAY

(A poem of inspiration)
Isaiah 40:29; Psalm 37:4, 5

Lord, help me make it through the day!
Let me be a contribution to someone along the way!

Please help me to encourage and exalt someone who feels
hopeless
To tell them of your joy
and happiness

That will lift them and bring fullness!
Let someone look at my face
and see a smile!
Let it give them strength in knowing
this day was all worthwhile!

SO GLAD

(A poem of protection)
Psalms 91; John 3:16,17

I am so glad that I am your child!
All the while, you have loved me.
The love you have is so amazing!
It's all my eyes could ever see!

Your love is endless and last always.
It gives me the strength to make it through the bleak days.

Your love is so sweet and so caring
You give your passion eagerly!

My life is so fulfilled in your love, far more than I thought it could
ever be!
You give your love so freely!

Who is this special one?
Who always watches you?
Who takes care of and protects you in all you do?

His name is awesome!
His name is Jesus!
My God, My Almighty Son!

HE CALLED ME

(A poem of rest and peace)
Proverbs 3:24; Matthew 11:28; Leviticus 26:6

I could hear my Father call
While I was in a deep sleep last night!
Move closer and enter! Into my perfect light!

Not a worry! Not a care!
Not a single burden to bear!

What a sweet presence of rest!
I have lived my very best!

Surprised, I know!
But don't cry for me!
Or worry, you see!

I am safe in my Savior's arms!
Where we all someday shall be!

LET ME ENTER

(A poem for Direction)
Isaiah 45:5; Revelation 1:8; John 14.6; Matthew 6:33; Psalms 32:8

Let me enter your life.
I need you, and you need me.
There's no one before me and no one after me.
I have a new way of life I want you to see!

My child, I am here today,
To give you instructions and direct your way!
I have called you by name!
Listen, I am Jesus; this is no game!

Read my word and seek my face!
Because I have so many precious things to give in these last
days.

It is your time to decide what you will do!
Will you serve me and have a life brand new?
I have many things planned for you. O yes, some things you thought
you never could do!
So, get ready, my child, and you will see. All the many blessings I
have for thee!

BLESSED WITH YOU

(A poem of blessings)
Isaiah 54:13, 14; Psalms 127:3; Genesis 22: 17, 18, 28: 14

Out of my womb,
God give me you!
My little boy,
My son brand new!

From a seed to a baby,
Form a baby to a boy,
From a boy to a man!
God is making you into his perfect plan!

I thank God for you!
But I give you back to him
That he may finish in you,
The work he has begun to do!

Dedicated to my son, Willie, Jr.

REVELATION

(A poem of revelation)
Amos 3: 7; I Corinthians 9:10; Proverbs 2:6, 7

God reveals His revelation. God springs up through me like fresh sweet water out of a well.

Let your powerful utterance of your Holy Spirit lead me into finding the mysteries you have revealed. Let me know the secrets of heaven. Which opens my spirit guiding and directing me into your perfect will?

Come and rest upon my heart until I feel peace. Your breath is a breeze upon my face.

Give me an understanding of your word that speaks into my heart that sounds aloud! But with such a calmness that is sweet as your spirit entering into my soul. Place just a finger upon my mind and fill me with wisdom, knowledge, and understanding that is clear, soft, and gentle as your loving touch.

Your words are as loud as a roaring lion sounding strong and mighty amid the earth. But yet I hear your voice so sweet and warm like a lamb calling me.

The Holy Spirit inside draws me close to you. It tells me of your power and anointing inside my vessel. Saying to me, "Servant, let me use you for My glory! I join in spirit with you within my body, mind, and soul, bringing peace that feasts my soul for everlasting life.

TEACH ME TO LOVE

(A poem of humility)
John 15:10, 12; 1 Chronicle 16:11; John 14:26
Dedicated to Aunt (Wren)

Lord, teach me to love
To love in every aspect of life!
Teach my soul and heart to
hold no strife!

Teach me to walk like You!
Teach me to talk like You!
Teach me to live like You!
Let my life shine in all
that I may say or do!

I will always seek Your face!
Thanking You continuously for
Your grace!
I will live each day,
Thanking Thee!
For Your awesome love
That You have given me

POEMS INDEX

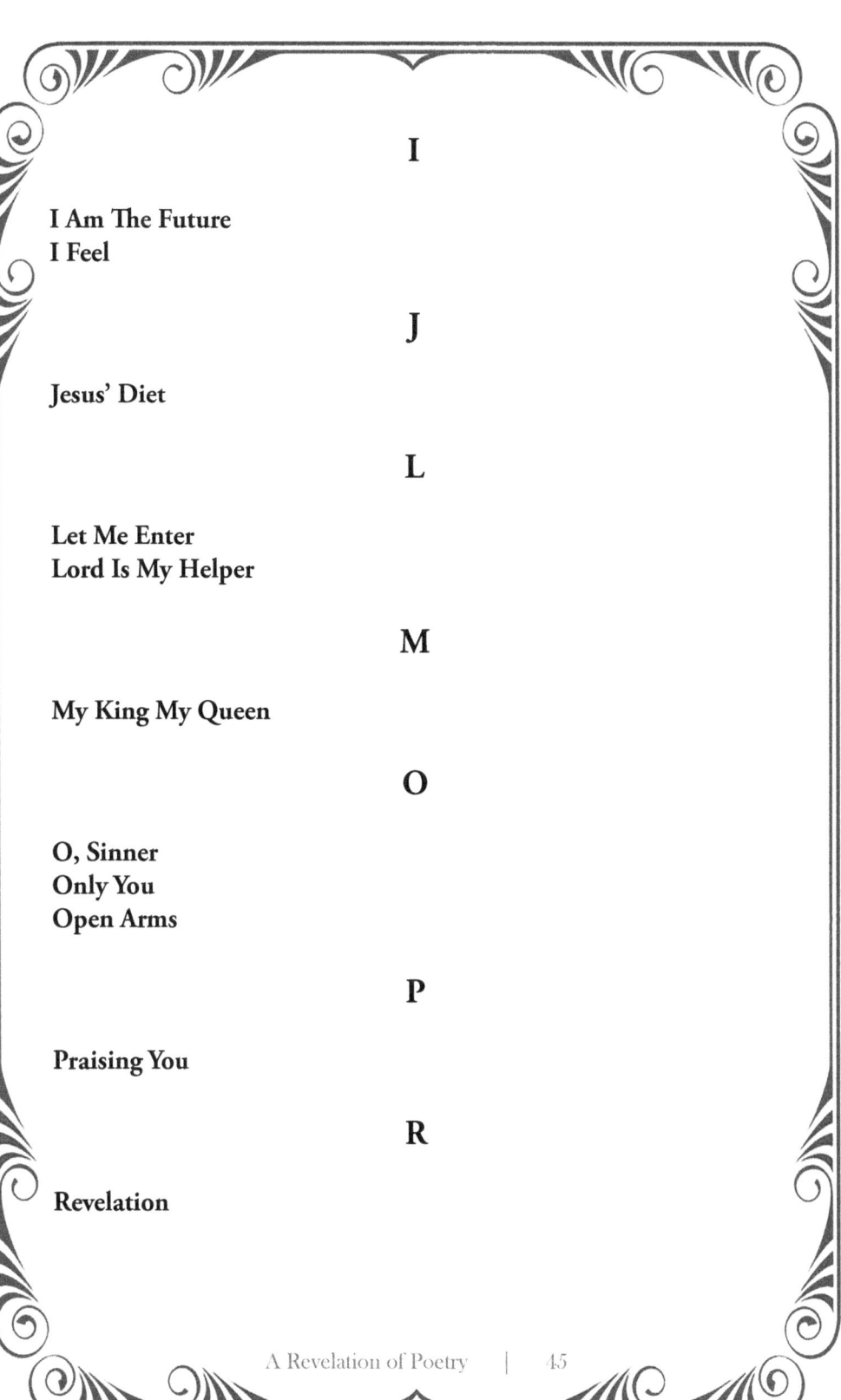

I

I Am The Future
I Feel

J

Jesus' Diet

L

Let Me Enter
Lord Is My Helper

M

My King My Queen

O

O, Sinner
Only You
Open Arms

P

Praising You

R

Revelation

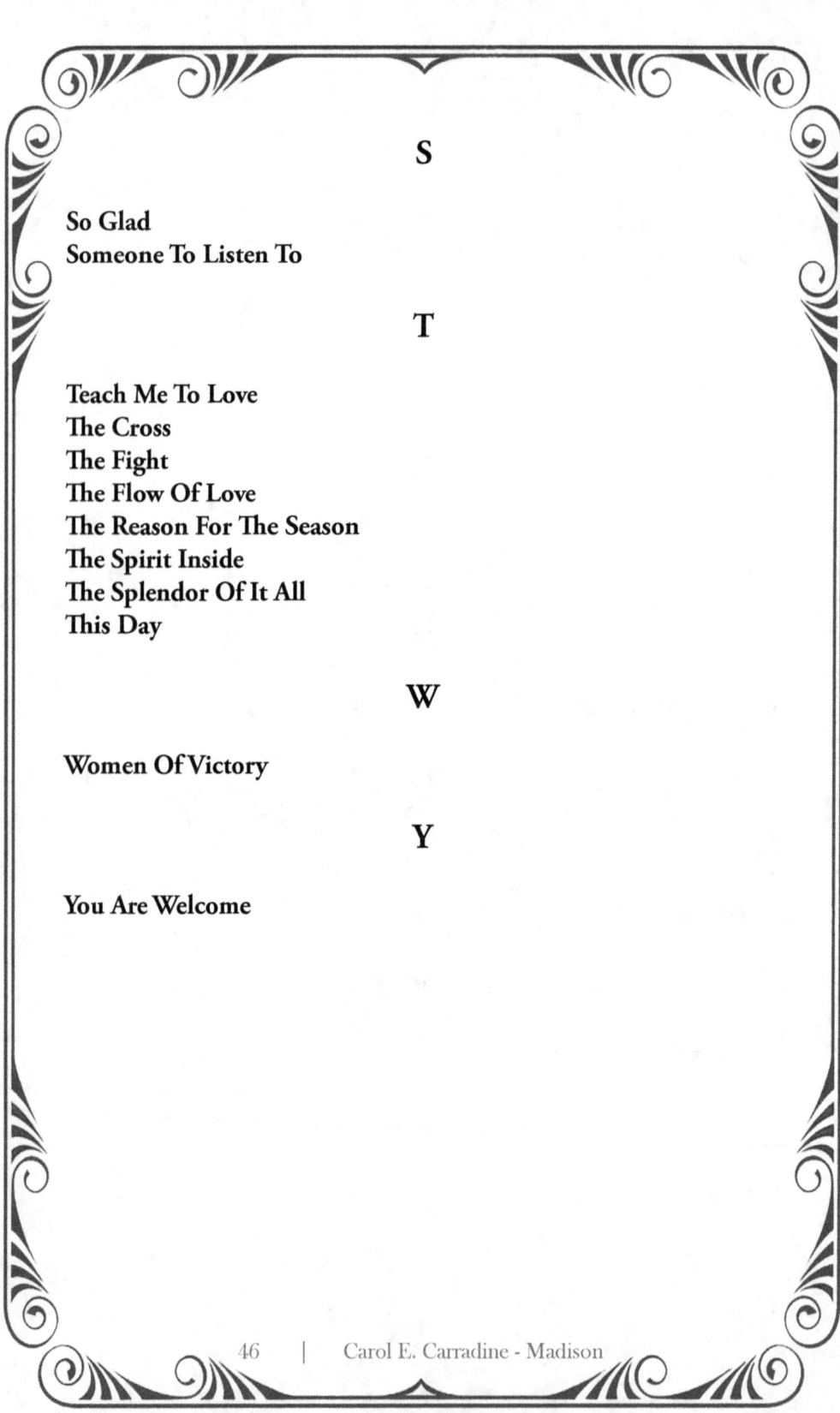

S

So Glad
Someone To Listen To

T

Teach Me To Love
The Cross
The Fight
The Flow Of Love
The Reason For The Season
The Spirit Inside
The Splendor Of It All
This Day

W

Women Of Victory

Y

You Are Welcome

ABOUT THE AUTHOR

Carol Elaine Carradine was born on August 27th. She was born in Wisner, LA, and spent most of her elementary and high school years there. After graduating high school, Carol attended the University of Louisiana Monroe for a year. After a year of college, she then met and married her husband and became a traveling military wife.

She and her family traveled worldwide, a once-in-a-lifetime experience, meeting different people and visiting various places. Many of the people she met turned out to become lifelong friends. Carol is a proud mother of two beautiful twin daughters and a handsome son. She is also the grandmother of six brilliant grandchildren and the great-grandmother of two adorable grandchildren. Carol and her husband decided to retire in New Orleans, Louisiana, where she lived for seventeen years and then relocated to Chicago for nine years.

Carol received an associate's degree in early childhood education while graduating with honors from Olive Harvey College. She spent nine years as a head start teacher for Chicago Public Schools; now, she has come full circle and is back in Louisiana. About twenty-five years ago, Carol realized her potential to write poetry. When teaching pre-school students in Atlanta, she proudly created a poem for them dedicated to Black History Month.

She recognized the untapped potential that God had awakened in her. So, Carol started allowing God to fill her up with this gift. Everything began to flow as she let him fill her heart with words, he would give her to write.

Carol gave the Revelation of Poetry its title because she genuinely believes it is a revelation from God and wrote this collection of poems over many years. This book has had its ups and downs, but now is the right time to bless it with others. Carol enjoys writing poetry because it relaxes her and allows her to express her feelings. She'll continue to write poetry as long as God gives her words to write.